A

Child's Guide

to

Pronunciation

Getting Ready to Read

Ann Marie Ireland

On Top of the World Press

Los Angeles

This book belongs to

_____

- -

_____

_____

- -

_____

First U.S. edition published in 1997 by
On Top of the World Press
Hollywood CA

www.ontopoftheworldpress.com

Copyright © 1997 by Ann Marie Ireland

Second printing 2005

Third printing 2012

Publisher's Cataloging in Publication

Ireland, Ann Marie
    A child's guide to pronunciation : getting ready to read / Ann Marie Ireland.
    p. cm.
    Includes index.
    Preassigned LCCN: 94-093916.
    ISBN: 978-1-884688-04-1

    1. English language—Pronunciation. I. Title.

PE1137.174 1996   428.1
                   QBI94-21206

Printed in the United States of America

To

Tom
who loved words

and

Delia Dagnault
who knew how to use them.

Nous serons de nouveau ensemble.

Bless the beasts
and the children,
for in this world
they have no voice,
they have no
choice.

Light their way
when the darkness
surrounds them.
Give them love,
let it shine all
around them.

Bless the beasts
and the children.
Give them shelter
from a storm.
Keep them safe,
keep them warm.

Thanks for the flowers, Moira.

You're an angel, Duke.

TABLE OF CONTENTS

A MESSAGE FROM THE AUTHOR

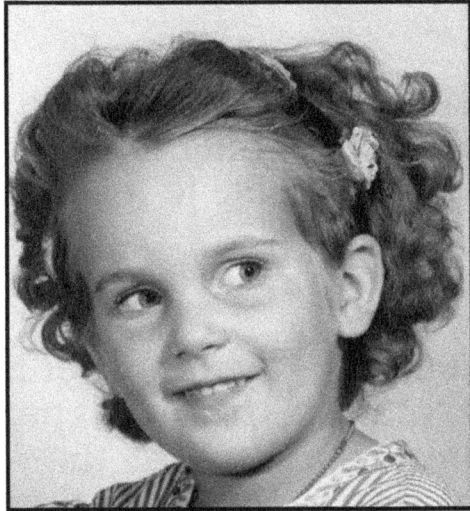

Dear Children,

Some of the happiest times of my childhood were spent listening to stories read to me by my family and then, later on, by my teachers in school.

The thought of learning how to read by myself was very exciting. I wanted to know how to turn all those letters in the alphabet into words. There was a secret about those letters and I wanted to know it.

The picture on this page is me. It shows how I looked when I first understood the secret. I knew it wouldn't be very long before I'd be able to read without any help.

What I'm going to tell you now is very special. It's what I know about the alphabet.

If you pay close attention and practice everything you're going to hear, you'll be on your way to being able to read all by yourself.

This is how it works. Here is the secret:

All the letters in the alphabet have a job to do. Each makes its own special sound. Some letters make more than one sound. When letters are put together they form words. Words form sentences. When sentences are put together they can become wonderful stories or give special information or tell how to do a job like baking a cake or fixing a bicycle.

So the secret to beginning to learn how to read is really very simple: Learn the sounds that each letter makes and you will be able to sound out almost every word you see.

There are two kinds of letters: consonants and vowels. The first part of this book tells about consonants and the sounds they make. The second part talks about vowels and the sounds they make.

Oops! I forgot to tell you another secret. Some words are special. They don't sound the way they look. They don't follow the rules. When you think about everything you will learn and you still can't sound out one of these words then there is only one thing to do: Go ask somebody. It's all right to get help while you're learning how to read.

Let's get started. Begin with the pages that tell you what the letters are and what sounds they usually make. If you already know lots of words then you might want to start further on.

Be patient. Although this book will give you lots of help, you must do the *thinking* yourself. When you start to sound out words without any help you will be on the way to discovering all the wonderful adventures to be found in books.

Have fun on your journey.

Your friend,

Ann Marie

One

THE ENGLISH ALPHABET

This is the English alphabet.
It contains 21 consonants and 5 vowels.

Aa   Bb   Cc   Dd

Ee   Ff   Gg   Hh   Ii

Jj   Kk   Ll   Mm

Nn   Oo   Pp   Qq   Rr

Ss   Tt   Uu   Vv

Ww   Xx   Yy   Zz

These are the consonants.

Bb Cc Dd Ff Gg

Hh Jj Kk Ll Mm

Nn Pp Qq Rr Ss Tt

Vv Ww Xx Yy Zz

These are the vowels.

Aa Ee Ii Oo Uu

Two

THE CONSONANTS

Consonants form the foundations of words. To correctly pronounce a word it is important to understand how consonants work. Each consonant in the alphabet makes at least one sound. Some of them make more than one. Learning to pronounce words would be a lot easier if each consonant made only one sound. Since there are more sounds than there are consonants, it is necessary to understand how they work and what sounds they make.

In the examples that follow, each word begins with a consonant and represents the sound or sounds of that consonant.

1. b-   bat   beg   bill   box   bud

2. c- = k   cab   cog   cub   cup

3. c- = s   cell   cent   cinch

4. d-   dad   den   dim   dog   dud

5. f-   fan   fed   fill   fog   fun

6. g-   gap   get   gill   got   gum

7. g- = j   gel   gem   gin

8. h-   hat   hem   hill   hot   hut

9. j-   jam   jet   jig   job   jug

10. k-   keg   kid   kin   kit

11. l-   lad   let   lip   lot   lug

12. m-   map   met   miss   mop   mug

13. n-　　nap　　net　　nix　　not　　nut

14. p-　　pat　　pen　　pill　　pot　　puff

15. qu- = kw　　quack　　quest　　quill

16. r-　　ran　　red　　rid　　rod　　rub

17. s-　　sap　　set　　sit　　sob　　sub

18. t-　　tab　　ten　　tip　　top　　tub

19. v-　　van　　vat　　vent　　vest　　vet

20. w-　　wag　　wax　　wed　　wet　　wig

21. x- = eks　　x-ray

22. x- = z　　xylophone

23. y-　　yak　　yap　　yell　　yip　　yup

24. z-　　zap　　zest　　zip

_____

- - - - - - - - - - - - - - - - -

_____

_____

- - - - - - - - - - - - - - - - -

_____

_____

- - - - - - - - - - - - - - - - -

_____

_____

- - - - - - - - - - - - - - - - -

_____

Three

CONSONANT BLENDS

Sometimes when two or more consonants are together they make a combined sound. This means the sound of each consonant can be heard as it blends with one or more consonants.

Two or more consonants together that make a combined sound are called blends.

Blends may be found at the beginning, in the middle and at the end of words.

The following 27 beginning and 16 ending blends are the ones in most common use. Usually these blends make the same sounds when found in the middle of words.

Beginning Blends

1. bl-

    black blend blimp block blunt

2. br-

    brand brick brig brim brunt

3. cl-

    class clench cliff clock clump

4. cr-

    crab crest crib crock crust

5. dr-

    draft dress drift drop drum

6. dw-

    dwarf dwell dwindle

7. fl-

    flap flex flip flop fluff

8. fr-

    frank   fret   frill   frog   frump

9. gl-

    glad   glen   glint   glob   glum

10. gr-

    grab   grill   grin   gruff   grumper

    grab   grill   grin   gruff   grump

11. pl-

    plan   plank   plink   plod   plot

12. pr-

    prank   prep   print   prod   prop

13. sc- = sk

    scamp   scan   scat   scoff   scuff

14. scr-

    scram   scrap   scrimp   script   scrub

15. sk-

skid   skim   skip   skit   skull

16. sl-

slab   sled   slim   slot   slush

17. sm-

smelt   smith   smock   smog   smug

18. sn-

snap   sniff   snip   snuff   snug

19. sp-

span   spell   spin   spot   spud

20. spl-

splash   splat   splint   split   splurge

21. spr-

sprain   sprat   sprig   sprint   sprout

22. squ- = skw

squelch   squid   squint   squish

23. st-

stamp   step   still   stop   stump

24. str-

strand   stress   strict   strum   strut

25. sw-

swell   swift   swig   swim   swish

26. tr-

track   trend   trip   trod   truck

27. tw-

twelve   twig   twin   twine   twist

Ending Blends

1. -ct

   act   fact   pact   tact   tract

2. -ft

   craft   gift   left   raft   soft

3. -ld

   bald   cold   held   meld   weld

4. -lf

   elf   self   shelf   wolf

5. -lk

   bulk   hulk   milk   silk

6. -lp

   gulp   help   kelp   scalp   whelp

7. -lt

   belt   bolt   felt   silt   stilt

8. -mp

bump   damp   jump   limp   slump

9. -mpt

attempt   exempt   prompt   tempt

10. -nd

bond   find   grand   land

11. -nt

ant   dent   font   pint   stunt

12. -pt

adopt   erupt   except   kept

13. -sk

ask   desk   mask   risk   task

14. -sp

clasp   gasp   grasp   hasp   rasp

15. -st

jest   last   mast   must   rest

Four

SILENT CONSONANTS

Sometimes when two or three
consonants are together, one or more
of the consonants are sounded and
the remainder are silent.

Silent consonants can be found
at the beginning, in the middle
and at the end of words.

The following beginning and ending
silent consonants are the ones
in most common use. Usually
they act the same way when
found in the middle of words.

Beginning Silent Consonants

1. gh- = g

   ghetto   ghost   ghoul

2. gn- = n

   gnarl   gnash   gnome   gnu

3. kn- = n

   knee   knit   knoll   knot

4. rh- = r

   rhapsody   rhinoceros   rhyme

5. sc- = s

   scent   science   scissors

6. wh- = h

   who   whole   whom   whose

7. wr- = r

   wrap   wren   wrist   write

Ending Silent Consonants

1. -ck = k

   crack   frock   luck   pick

2. -ght = t

   night   right   slight   tight

3. -gn = n

   align   benign   design   sign

4. -ld = d

   could   should   would

5. -lk = k

   chalk   talk   walk   yolk

6. -lm = m

   balm   calm   palm   qualm

7. -mb = m

   climb   crumb   numb   plumb

Five

UNUSUAL CONSONANT COMBINATIONS

The following consonant combinations
are each unusual in some way.
Some of the consonants are silent.
Some of them make the sound
of a different consonant.
Some of them work together
to make a new sound.

These consonant combinations
usually make the same sounds
whether found at the beginning,
middle or end of a word.

Beginning Consonants

1. ch- = k

   chemical   chord   chorus

2. ch- = sh

   chagrin   charade   chef   chute

3. chl- = kl

   chlorine   chloroform   chlorophyll

4. chr- = kr

   chrome   chronic   chrysalis

5. ph- = f

   phase   phobia   phone   photo

6. sch- = sk

   scheme   scholar   school   schooner

7. shr-

   shred   shrimp   shrink   shrub

8. thr-

    thrift   thrill   throb   thrust

Ending Consonants

1. -gh = f

    cough   enough   rough

2. -gh = g̶h̶

    high   sigh   though   weigh

3. -ght = t

    freight   straight   weight

4. -nch

    branch   inch   lunch   ranch

5. -ng

hang   king   long   sting

6. -nk

bank   dunk   slink   tank

7. -nth

eleventh   month   ninth   tenth

8. -ph = f

holograph   paragraph   telegraph

9. -tch = ch

catch   crutch   glitch   notch

Some consonant combinations are very rare. They form just one or two words. These words are well-known.

Beginning Consonants

1. kh- = k
   khaki

2. kr-
   krill

3. phr- = fr
   phrase

4. sph- = sf
   sphere   sphinx

5. sw- = s
   sword

6. wh- = w
   wharf

Ending Consonants

1. -bt = t
   debt   doubt

2. -ch = k
   stomach

3. -ngth
   length   strength

4. -xt
   next   text

Six

THE SOUNDS OF
ch AND *sh* AND *wh*

The following pairs of consonants create combined sounds. These sounds are not the same as those that would be heard if each letter were sounded separately.

1. ch-

   chain   champ   charm   chest

   chin   chop   chuck   chunk

2. -ch

   beach   coach   leach   peach

   preach   reach   speech   teach

3. sh-

   shack   shade   shave   shed

   shift   shine   shop   shore

4. -sh

brush	cash	flash	fresh
hash	plush	rash	wish

5. wh-

wheat	wheel	whiff	while
whim	whir	whisk	whiz

The consonant pair *wh* is not found at the end of words.

Seven

THE SOUNDS OF *th*

Whether at the beginning or the end
of a word, *th* can have two sounds.
These sounds are called
unvoiced and voiced.

The unvoiced sound of *th*
at the beginning of words:

1. thank
2. thatch
3. thaw
4. theme
5. thick
6. thin
7. think
8. third
9. thirst
10. thong
11. thumb
12. thump

The unvoiced sound of *th*
at the end of words:

1. booth
2. breath
3. broth
4. earth
5. fourth
6. hearth
7. moth
8. north
9. path
10. south
11. teeth
12. tooth

The voiced sound of *th*
at the beginning of words:

1. than   2. that   3. the

4. them   5. then   6. they

7. this   8. those   9. thus

The voiced sound of *th* at the
end of words, as in smooth, is
not very common.

Both the unvoiced and the voiced
sounds of *th* can be found
in the middle of many words.

1. brother   2. ether   3. father

4. mother   5. nothing   6. panther

Eight

DOUBLE CONSONANTS

Usually when two of the same consonants are together, they make just one sound.

Double consonants may be found in the middle of words.

1. blizzard	2. burro	3. clipper
4. corral	5. gallop	6. kennel
7. possum	8. rabbit	9. rubber
10. saddle	11. slipper	12. snuggle
13. traffic	14. upper	15. village
16. waddle	17. wiggle	18. yellow

Double consonants may be found at the end of words.

1. bell
2. bless
3. bluff
4. buff
5. burr
6. buzz
7. cress
8. dill
9. drill
10. egg
11. jell
12. press
13. shell
14. tell
15. till
16. toss
17. well
18. will

Llama is the only well-known
word that begins with
the same two consonants.

Nine

s AND t

s and t sometimes make the sounds
of other consonants.

The consonant s can sound like z.

1. amuse	2. busy	3. chose
4. close	5. cousin	6. desert
7. drowsy	8. hose	9. laser
10. lens	11. nose	12. pose

The consonants tt can sound like d.

1. bitter	2. blotter	3. butter
4. cattle	5. clutter	6. critter
7. flutter	8. gutter	9. letter
10. litter	11. platter	12. scatter

Ten

THE VOWELS

a, *e*, *i*, *o* and *u* are the vowels.

The sound of a vowel is the most important sound in a word. Understanding how vowels work and the various sounds they produce make it possible to pronounce most words.

Words cannot be made of consonants alone. Every word must have at least one sounded vowel. Just as consonants can be silent, vowels can also be silent.

w and *y* can sometimes act as vowels. *w* can take the place of *u*. *y* can take the place of *e* or *i*.

Just as some consonants can
make more than one sound, each vowel
can also make more than one sound.

Each vowel has a short sound and
a long sound. When two vowels are
together, usually one is sounded
and the other is silent. Sometimes
when two vowels are together they
form a new sound. The sounds of
vowels can be changed when
followed by certain consonants.

Once the different sounds of *a*, *e*, *i*,
o and *u* are understood, unlocking
the correct pronunciation of
most words becomes possible.

Eleven

SHORT VOWEL SOUNDS

The short sound of a vowel is
its most common sound.

This is the way vowels with
a short sound are marked:

ă ĕ ĭ ŏ ŭ

The short sound of *a* is ă as in cat.

cat

The short sound of *e* is ĕ as in hen.

hen

The short sound of *i* is ĭ as in pig.

pig

The short sound of *o* is ŏ as in fox.

fox

The short sound of *u* is ŭ as in duck.

duck

ă

The vowel sound in each of the following words is short.

Remember:

a usually sounds like ă as in cat.

1. am	2. ash	3. at
4. back	5. bask	6. blast
7. bran	8. can	9. dash
10. flat	11. glass	12. grass
13. hand	14. mat	15. plant
16. ramp	17. shaft	18. stand
19. tan	20. tramp	21. vast

ĕ

The vowel sound in each of the following words is short.

Remember:

e usually sounds like ĕ as in hen.

1. bend	2. best	3. deck
4. end	5. flesh	6. less
7. men	8. mend	9. neck
10. nest	11. sent	12. speck
13. stem	14. swept	15. tent
16. test	17. trench	18. went
19. west	20. yes	21. yet

ĭ

The vowel sound in each of the following words is short.

Remember:

i usually sounds like ĭ as in pig.

1. big	2. chick	3. click
4. clip	5. fin	6. fit
7. lift	8. list	9. mint
10. mist	11. rich	12. ship
13. skill	14. skin	15. stick
16. tick	17. tin	18. trick
19. trim	20. wick	21. wind

ŏ

The vowel sound in each of the
following words is short.

Remember:

o usually sounds like ŏ as in fox.

1. bob   2. cost   3. crop

4. cross   5. flock   6. frost

7. jog   8. josh   9. loft

10. lost   11. moss   12. nod

13. off   14. pond   15. pop

16. rock   17. romp   18. shock

19. slosh   20. song   21. tom

ŭ

The vowel sound in each of the
following words is short.

Remember:

u usually sounds like ŭ as in duck.

1. bug	2. club	3. dump
4. fund	5. hug	6. junk
7. just	8. mud	9. munch
10. plum	11. pulp	12. rug
13. run	14. stuck	15. stuff
16. such	17. sum	18. sun
19. trust	20. tusk	21. us

Twelve

LONG VOWEL SOUNDS
IN WORDS THAT END WITH *e*

The short sound of a vowel is the most
frequently heard vowel sound in
words. There are times, however,
when vowels do not make this sound.
The next most common sound
of a vowel is its long sound.

The long sound of a vowel is the
same as the name of that vowel.

Some words end with an *e*
and contain one other vowel.
Usually in these words, the final *e*
is silent and the other vowel
makes its long sound.

If a word that ends with a
silent *e* contains more than one
other vowel, usually at least one
of those vowels makes its long sound.

This is the way vowels with
a long sound are marked:

ā ē ī ō ū

The long sound of *a* is ā as in whale.

whale

The long sound of *e* is ē as in athlete.

athlete

The long sound of *i* is ī as in smile.

smile

The long sound of *o* is ō as in rose.

rose

The long sound of *u* is ū as in mule.

mule

Each of the following words contains
a long vowel sound and ends
with a silent *e*.

a sounds like ā as in whale.
The final *e* is silent.

1. bake   2. cave   3. gave

4. lake   5. place   6. race

7. safe   8. shape   9. state

10. take   11. trade   12. wave

e sounds like ē as in athlete.
The final *e* is silent.

1. compete   2. complete   3. concrete

4. delete   5. stampede   6. scene

One-syllable words that contain
a long *e* and end with a consonant and
a silent *e* are not very common.

i sounds like ī as in smile.
The final *e* is silent.

1. chime 2. drive 3. fine

4. life 5. live 6. mile

7. pine 8. quite 9. ride

10. size 11. time 12. wide

o sounds like ō as in rose.
The final *e* is silent.

1. bone 2. globe 3. home

4. hope 5. note 6. pole

7. rode 8. rope 9. stone

10. stove 11. tone 12. tote

u sounds like ū as in mule.
The final *e* is silent.

1. cute	2. duke	3. flute
4. fuse	5. jute	6. lute
7. mute	8. prude	9. prune
10. rule	11. tube	12. tune

Thirteen

MORE LONG VOWEL SOUNDS

Words do not need to end with an
e to contain a long vowel.

An *i* that comes just before -ght
is usually long.

1. bright   2. flight   3. knight

4. might   5. plight   6. sight

An *i* that comes just before -ld
is usually long.

1. child   2. mild   3. wild

An *i* that comes just before -nd
is usually long.

1. bind   2. blind   3. grind

4. kind   5. mind   6. wind

An *o* that comes just before -ld
is usually long.

1. bold   2. fold   3. gold

4. hold   5. mold   6. sold

An *o* that comes just before -ll
is usually long.

1. boll   2. poll   3. roll

4. stroll   5. toll   6. troll

An *o* that comes before -st
is usually long.

1. co̸a̸st   2. host   3. most

4. post   5. ro̸a̸st   6. to̸a̸st

Fourteen

DIGRAPHS

A digraph is two vowels together,
one sounded and one silent,
or two vowels together making
the sound of a different vowel.

There are five types of digraphs.

Digraph One

The first vowel makes its long sound.
The second vowel is silent.

bo̅a̸t

Digraph Two

The first vowel makes its short sound.
The second vowel is silent.

lă**u**gh

Digraph Three

The first vowel is silent.
The second vowel makes its long sound.

ch**i**̄ef

Digraph Four

The first vowel is silent.
The second vowel makes its short sound.

fr*ĭ*end

Digraph Five

The digraph makes the sound of a different vowel.

ā
sleigh

Examples of Digraphs

Digraph One

The first vowel makes its long sound.
The second vowel is silent.

1. beam   2. dream   3. feast

4. fruit   5. heat   6. lead

7. main   8. meal   9. paint

10. read   11. road   12. suit

Digraph Two

The first vowel makes its short sound.
The second vowel is silent.

1. bread   2. broad   3. deaf

4. head   5. health   6. lead

7. meant   8. read   9. spread

10. thread   11. tread   12. wealth

Digraph Three

The first vowel is silent.
The second vowel makes its long sound.

1. break   2. brief   3. field

4. great   5. group   6. piece

7. shield   8. shriek   9. soup

10. wound   11. yield   12. youth

Digraph Four

The first vowel is silent.
The second vowel makes its short sound.

1. biscuit   2. build   3. captain

4. circuit   5. country   6. double

7. famous   8. guess   9. guest

10. guild   11. touch   12. young

Digraph Five

The digraph makes the
sound of a different vowel.

1. boot   2. broom   3. fawn

4. flood   5. food   6. haul

7. moon   8. pigeon   9. rein

10. rooster   11. room   12. vein

Remember: A digraph is either two vowels together, one sounded and one silent; or two vowels together making the sound of a different vowel.

There are times, however, when two vowels are together and both are sounded. These are not digraphs.

The two vowels may each
make their long sound.

One may be long and the other short.

One or both vowels may make
the sound of another vowel.

Remember:
The following vowel pairs *are not* digraphs.

1. client   2. create   3. diet

4. duet   5. duo   6. fiesta

7. meander   8. medium   9. mosaic

10. neon   11. oasis   12. oriole

13. patio   14. piano   15. radio

16. trio   17. utopia   18. video

19. violet   20. violin   21. zinnia

Fifteen

DIPHTHONGS

Usually when *o* is followed by
i, u, w or *y* the two vowels
combine to make one new sound. These
vowel combinations are called diphthongs.

Diphthongs can be found at
the beginning, in the middle
and at the end of words.

These are the four diphthongs:

oi   oy   ou   ow

This is the way they are marked:

oi   oy   ou   ow

When *oi* is a diphthong,
it sounds like (oi) as in coin.

coin

When *oy* is a diphthong,
it sounds like (oy) as in boy.

boy

When *ou* is a diphthong,
it sounds like (ou) as in house.

house

When *ow* is a diphthong,
it sounds like (ow) as in cow.

cow

Examples of Diphthongs

oi sounds like Ⓞⓘ as in coin.

1. boil   2. broil   3. coil

4. foil   5. join   6. moist

7. oil   8. oink   9. soil

10. spoil 11. toil   12. voice

oy sounds like Ⓞⓨ as in boy.

1. convoy 2. coy   3. decoy

4. employ 5. joy   6. loyal

7. oyster 8. ploy   9. royal

10. soy   11. toy   12. voyage

ou sounds like ⓞⓤ as in house.

1. blouse   2. cloud   3. count

4. found   5. ground   6. hound

7. mouth   8. ounce   9. pounce

10. round   11. trout   12. wound

ow sounds like ⓞⓦ as in cow.

1. bow   2. brown   3. clown

4. down   5. gown   6. growl

7. howl   8. jowl   9. owl

10. plow   11. sow   12. town

Sometimes *ow* does not sound like the *ow* in cow and so it is not a diphthong.

The *ow* in each of the following words is not a diphthong because the vowel sound is a long *o* and the *w* is silent.

1. blow 　　 2. bow 　　 3. crow

4. flow 　　 5. glow 　　 6. grow

7. low 　　 8. mow 　　 9. row

10. slow 　　 11. snow 　　 12. sow

13. stow 　　 14. throw 　　 15. tow

Sixteen

A NEW SOUND FOR
oo AND *u*

Sometimes *oo* and *u* make a new
sound. This sound is the sound
heard in the word *cook*.

cook

Here are some examples
of this new sound:

1. book   2. brook   3. bull

4. bush   5. crook   6. foot

7. full   8. good   9. hood

10. hoof   11. hook   12. nook

13. pull   14. push   15. put

16. roof   17. rook   18. shook

19. soot   20. stood   21. took

22. wood   23. woof   24. wool

Seventeen

ROLLING VOWELS®

A rolling vowel is a vowel whose
sound is changed by the *r*
that follows it.

This is the way
rolling vowels are marked:

(ar)   (er)   (ir)   (or)   (ur)

When *ar* is a rolling vowel,
it sounds like (ar) as in farm.

farm

When *er* is a rolling vowel, it sounds like ⓔⓡ as in herd.

herd

When *ir* is a rolling vowel, it sounds like ⓘⓡ as in girl.

girl

When *or* is a rolling vowel,
it sounds like (or) as in horse.

horse

When *ur* is a rolling vowel,
it sounds like (ur) as in church.

church

Examples of Rolling Vowels®

ar sounds like (ar) as in farm.

1.	arm	2.	chart	3.	dark
4.	dart	5.	march	6.	mark
7.	mart	8.	park	9.	part
10.	sharp	11.	star	12.	yard

er sounds like (er) as in herd.

1.	berth	2.	clerk	3.	fern
4.	germ	5.	her	6.	perk
7.	river	8.	sister	9.	tender
10.	term	11.	verse	12.	whisper

ir sounds like (ir) as in girl.

1. birth 2. firm 3. flirt

4. girth 5. mirth 6. shirt

7. sir 8. skirt 9. squirm

10. stir 11. twirl 12. whirl

or sounds like (or) as in horse.

1. born 2. cord 3. corn

4. form 5. fort 6. forth

7. porch 8. port 9. scorch

10. stork 11. thorn 12. torch

ur sounds like (ur) as in church.

1. burn   2. burst   3. churn

4. curb   5. curl   6. fur

7. lurch   8. lurk   9. nurse

10. purr   11. surf   12. turn

Notice that *er*, *ir* and *ur*
make the same sound.

1. stern   2. bird   3. slurp

Sometimes *re* sounds like (er).

For example:

1. acre   2. fire   3. hire

4. mire   5. tire   6. wire

Eighteen

TWO SPECIAL SOUNDS

In some words *-air*, *-are*, *-ear*, *-eir*
and *-ere* sound like <u>air</u>.

bear

Each of the following words
contains this sound.

1. care   2. fair   3. fare

4. hair   5. mare   6. pare

7. pear   8. stare   9. tear

10. their   11. there   12. where

In some words *-ear*, *-eer*, *-eir*, *-ere*
and *-ier* sound like <u>ear</u>.

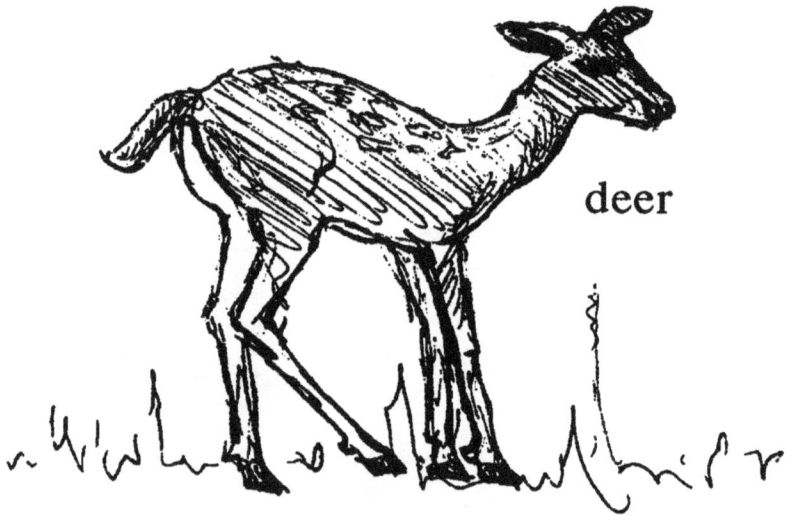

deer

Each of the following words
contains this sound.

1. clear   2. dear   3. gear

4. hear   5. here   6. near

7. peer   8. pier   9. sheer

10. tear   11. weird   12. year

Nineteen

ABOUT THE VOWEL *a*

The most common sound of the vowel
a is its short sound. Remember that
a usually sounds like ă as in cat.

The sound of *a* that is the easiest
to remember is its long sound.
This sound is the same as the
name of the vowel. An example
of this is the sound of *a* in whale.

Here are two other sounds
that the vowel *a* makes:

tall

a sounds like a short *o* in the
word tall. Therefore the
a in tall sounds like ŏ.

zebra

a sounds like a short *u* in the
word zebra. Therefore the
a in zebra sounds like ŭ.

The *a* in each of the following words is making either the sound of a short *o* or the sound of a short *u*.

1. across   2. ago   3. alike

4. alive   5. almost   6. along

7. also   8. awhile   9. extra

10. finally   11. flaw   12. hall

13. purchase   14. salt   15. soda

16. sofa   17. stall   18. straw

19. surface   20. swab   21. swamp

22. swan   23. swap   24. tuna

25. tundra   26. wall   27. wallow

28. waltz   29. want   30. watt

Here is an example of these two sounds of *a* in the same word:

lava

Twenty

w AND *y* AS VOWELS

Both *w* and *y* can take the place of vowels.
w takes the place of long *u* when it
acts as a vowel. *y* takes the place
of *e* or *i* when it acts as a vowel.

Sometimes *w* sounds like ū as in ewe.
This is the long *u* sound.

ewe

$w = \bar{u}$

1. blew	2. chew	3. crew
4. dew	5. drew	6. few
7. flew	8. grew	9. mew
10. stew	11. strew	12. view

Sometimes *y* sounds like ĭ as in nymph.
This is the short *i* sound.

nymph

$$y = ĭ$$

1. crypt   2. crystal   3. cylinder

4. cymbal   5. gym   6. hymn

7. mystic   8. myth   9. oxygen

Sometimes *y* sounds like ī as in sky.
This is the long *i* sound.

sky

$y = ī$

1. by   2. cry   3. dry   4. fly

5. fry   6. guy   7. ply   8. pry

9. shy   10. sly   11. spry   12. spy

Sometimes *y* sounds like ē as in baby. This usually happens when there is more than one syllable in a word. This is the long *e* sound.

baby

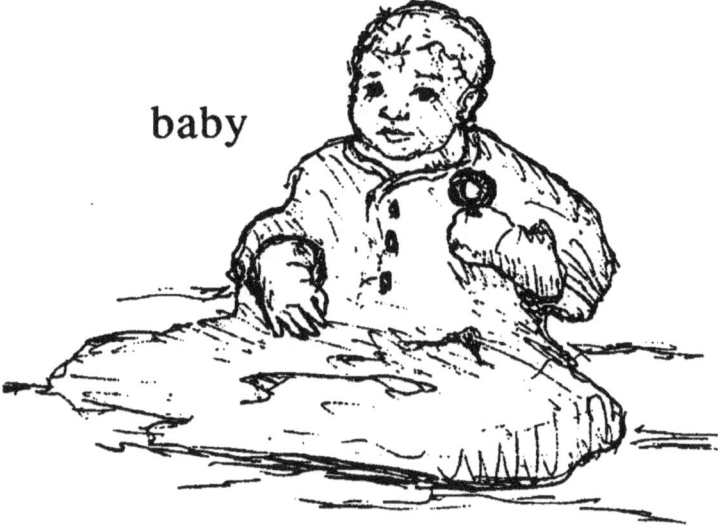

$y = \bar{e}$

1. army   2. copy   3. early

4. happy   5. jelly   6. lady

7. party   8. puppy   9. story

10. study   11. tabby   12. tiny

Twenty-one

i AND *u* AS CONSONANTS

Sometimes *i* takes the place of *y*.
When it does it makes the sound
of the consonant *y*.

In each of the following examples
-*ion* sounds like -*yun*.

$$i = y$$

1. billion   2. dominion   3. grunion

4. million   5. onion   6. opinion

7. trillion   8. union   9. zillion

When *u* follows *q* it makes the sound of the consonant *w*.

$$u = w$$

1. quail   2. quaint   3. quake

4. queen   5. quell   6. quench

7. quick   8. quiet   9. quilt

10. quint   11. quip   12. quirk

13. quit   14. quiz   15. quote

Twenty-two

THE INVISIBLE VOWEL®

When *-le* follows a consonant
and is at the end of a word,
the final *e* is silent.

This *-le* ending and the
consonant that comes before it
are the last syllable of the word.

The sound of a short *u* is heard
in this syllable and comes from
between the last two consonants.

people

Each of the following words
ends with an *-le* and contains the
invisible short *u* sound.

1. able   2. angle   3. ankle

4. apple   5. bubble   6. candle

7. circle   8. cycle   9. eagle

10. gentle   11. handle   12. jungle

13. peddle   14. puddle   15. purple

16. puzzle   17. riddle   18. shuffle

19. simple   20. single   21. sparkle

22. table   23. turtle   24. twinkle

Twenty-three

WORDS THAT END IN
-*sion* AND -*tion*

Usually -*sion* and -*tion* sound like *shun*.
The vowel sound here is a short *u*.

mansion

pollution

-tion and *-sion* sound like *shun*
in these words.

1. action   2. addition   3. condition

4. direction   5. fraction   6. invention

7. mission   8. reception   9. session

Notice the *shun* sound here.

ocean

Sometimes *-tion* and *-sion* sound like *zhun*.

1. confusion   2. decision   3. division

4. equation   5. illusion   6. vision

-tion sounds like *chun* in *question*.

Twenty-four

MIXED VOWEL SOUNDS

These words contain more than one vowel
and more than one vowel sound. Some
vowel sounds are long and some are short.
Some words contain rolling vowels.
Some words contain diphthongs.
Some words contain digraphs.

1. acorn
2. after
3. beautiful

4. cactus
5. closet
6. counter

7. crayon
8. divide
9. feather

10. flower
11. guitar
12. hammer

13. leader
14. magnet
15. number

16. ostrich
17. poem
18. program

19. pumpkin
20. ruler
21. silver

22. spider
23. valentine
24. winter

Here are more words with mixed vowel sounds.

1. absent
2. acrobat
3. barber
4. bumper
5. carpenter
6. chimney
7. diner
8. dinner
9. elbow
10. explore
11. forest
12. helmet
13. holiday
14. insect
15. jacket
16. journey
17. lobster
18. lonely
19. magic
20. napkin
21. peanut
22. plastic
23. reptile
24. robot
25. shadow
26. summer
27. teacher
28. tower
29. unicorn
30. window

Twenty-five

EXCEPTIONS

Exceptions are words that contain
at least one letter that does not
make its usual sound.

One example of an exception is angel
because both the *a* and the *e* should be
making their short sounds. Instead
a is long and *e* sounds like short u.

angel

Each of the following words is an exception.
Remember that each word contains at
least one vowel or consonant that
doesn't make its usual sound.

1. alarm   2. armor   3. ball

4. become   5. bloom   6. cereal

7. color   8. cover   9. crawl

10. doctor   11. dove   12. elephant

13. exhaust   14. flour   15. front

16. giant   17. harbor   18. laundry

19. lawn   20. minute   21. money

22. movie   23. person   24. salad

25. second   26. shoe   27. sponge

28. tomato   29. won   30. world

Here are more exceptions.

1. amount   2. animal   3. area

4. balloon   5. cafe   6. cashier

7. dollar   8. faucet   9. gauze

10. glove   11. happen   12. honey

13. human   14. idea   15. library

16. lion   17. lizard   18. motor

19. oval   20. picture   21. prove

22. reward   23. shovel   24. solar

25. son   26. theater   27. wagon

28. watch   29. woman   30. yawn

The most well-known exception of all:

love

Twenty-six

GO ASK SOMEBODY

Sometimes words can be sounded out even if they are exceptions. However when words cannot be easily sounded out it is a good idea to *go ask somebody* for help.

The following words are very special. Usually help will be necessary to unlock their pronunciation.

1. almond
2. another
3. answer

4. applaud
5. blanket
6. calf

7. caught
8. century
9. choir

10. clothes
11. courage
12. daughter

13. depot
14. dictionary
15. dinosaur

16. eye

17. figure

18. future

19. genius

20. half

21. hanger

22. honest

23. honor

24. hour

25. iron

26. ketchup

27. kitchen

28. knew

29. lamb

30. limb

31. listen

32. measure

33. mirror

34. nature

35. neighbor

36. none

37. often

38. paw

39. pitcher

40. pour

41. receipt

42. recipe

43. routine

44. sentence

45. soldier

46. sour

47. special

48. squad

49. square

50. sugar

51. sure

Twenty-seven

WHAT DO YOU *THINK*?

Just looking at words *without thinking*
will not unlock their pronunciation.
You must use your *brain*.
You must *think*.

If you went through this book carefully
you now know enough about vowels and
consonants to sound out most words.

Here are five steps to take each
time you see a new word. The first
three must be done silently.

1. Look at the word. Think of another
    word that starts the same way.

2. Look at the vowels.

*3. Think of the sounds the vowels
     probably make.

4. Say the sound of each vowel.

5. Say the word.

*How to think about the vowels:

Are they

1. short?
2. long?
3. digraphs?
4. diphthongs?
5. Rolling Vowels®?
6. exceptions?

If you try everything you've learned
about vowels and consonants and you
still can't sound out the word
GO ASK SOMEBODY for help.

Twenty-eight

LEARN THESE BY HEART

The following words must be known by sight before the process of learning how to read can begin.

1. a   2. about   3. above

4. again   5. all   6. always

7. any   8. around   9. as

10. away   11. because   12. been

13. better   14. both   15. bring

16. buy   17. call   18. carry

19. come   20. could   21. day

22. do   23. does   24. done

25. draw   26. drink   27. eight

28. every   29. fall   30. from

31. full	32. goes	33. going
34. gone	35. good	36. has
37. have	38. here	39. hers
40. his	41. into	42. know
43. laugh	44. light	45. little
46. live	47. long	48. look
49. many	50. may	51. move
52. my	53. new	54. of
55. once	56. one	57. only
58. open	59. other	60. our
61. own	62. people	63. please
64. pretty	65. pull	66. put
67. right	68. said	69. saw
70. say	71. says	72. seven
73. sing	74. small	75. some

76. soon	77. than	78. thank
79. that	80. the	81. their
82. them	83. then	84. there
85. these	86. they	87. think
88. this	89. those	90. three
91. to	92. today	93. together
94. too	95. two	96. us
97. use	98. very	99. walk
100. want	101. warm	102. was
103. wash	104. water	105. way
106. were	107. what	108. when
109. where	110. which	111. white
112. who	113. why	114. with
115. word	116. work	117. would
118. write	119. you	120. your

Twenty-nine

SOME USEFUL INFORMATION

Colors

1. black	7. pink
2. blue	8. purple
3. brown	9. red
4. gray	10. white
5. green	11. yellow
6. orange	

Shapes

1. circle
2. oval
3. rectangle
4. square
5. triangle

Seasons

1. summer
2. winter
3. spring
4. fall

Days of the Week

1. Sunday
2. Monday
3. Tuesday
4. Wednesday
5. Thursday
6. Friday
7. Saturday

Months of the Year

1. January	5. May	9. September
2. February	6. June	10. October
3. March	7. July	11. November
4. April	8. August	12. December

Numbers
(cardinal)

1. one	16. sixteen
2. two	17. seventeen
3. three	18. eighteen
4. four	19. nineteen
5. five	20. twenty
6. six	21. twenty-one
7. seven	22. twenty-two
8. eight	23. twenty-three
9. nine	24. twenty-four
10. ten	25. twenty-five
11. eleven	26. twenty-six
12. twelve	27. twenty-seven
13. thirteen	28. twenty-eight
14. fourteen	29. twenty-nine
15. fifteen	30. thirty

More Numbers
(ordinal)

1. first	6. sixth
2. second	7. seventh
3. third	8. eighth
4. fourth	9. ninth
5. fifth	10. tenth

Antonyms (opposite)		Synonyms (same)	
1. above	below	1. ancient	old
2. all	none	2. auto	car
3. always	never	3. begin	start
4. back	front	4. big	huge
5. big	little	5. build	make
6. borrow	loan	6. close	shut
7. cold	hot	7. cluster	group
8. dark	light	8. correct	right
9. day	night	9. earth	world
10. found	lost	10. enjoy	like
11. hard	soft	11. gallop	run
12. heavy	light	12. go	leave
13. high	low	13. grow	raise
14. large	small	14. high	tall
15. left	right	15. keep	save
16. new	old	16. kind	nice
17. no	yes	17. little	tiny
18. off	on	18. lock	seal
19. over	under	19. look	stare
20. play	work	20. memo	note
21. receive	send	21. name	title
22. remove	replace	22. ocean	sea
23. run	walk	23. photo	picture
24. sour	sweet	24. place	put
25. start	stop	25. say	speak

Homonyms
(same sounds, different meanings)

		Compound Words
1. ant	aunt	1. airport
2. ate	eight	2. anteater
3. berry	bury	3. blackberry
4. blew	blue	4. butterfly
5. brake	break	5. campfire
6. cent	scent	6. dashboard
7. close	clothes	7. drawbridge
8. doe	dough	8. eyeglasses
9. flour	flower	9. fireworks
10. gnu	new	10. grasshopper
11. hair	hare	11. haystack
12. heal	heel	12. inchworm
13. main	mane	13. jawbone
14. pail	pale	14. ladybug
15. peak	peek	15. lighthouse
16. road	rode	16. mockingbird
17. son	sun	17. overgrown
18. stair	stare	18. pineapple
19. tail	tale	19. playground
20. toe	tow	20. rainbow
21. vane	vein	21. scarecrow
22. waist	waste	22. sunset
23. wait	weight	23. swordfish
24. weak	week	24. tugboat
25. yoke	yolk	25. windmill

Thirty

A FEW WORDS ABOUT
THE ALPHABET

The alphabet that is on pages 17 and
18 shows how letters look when
they are printed in books. This is not the
way they will look when it is time
to learn how to print them.

It is very important that letters be
printed carefully so that they are easy to read.
On the next page is an alphabet that can be
used to learn to print. It shows how each
letter is formed. Anyone who practices these
letters carefully will soon be able
to print very well.

Aa Bb Cc

Dd Ee Ff

Gg Hh Ii Jj

Kk Ll Mm

Nn Oo Pp

Qq Rr Ss Tt

Uu Vv Ww

Xx Yy Zz

INDEX

126

Note: The words from pages 119 through 122 are not included here.

a 115
able 102
about 115
above 115
absent 106
acorn 105
acre 90
acrobat 106
across 94
act 28
action 104
addition 104
adopt 29
after 105
again 115
ago 94
alarm 108
align 33
alike 94
alive 94
all 115
almond 111
almost 94
along 94
also 94
always 115
am 54
amount 109
amuse 47
angel 107
angle 102
animal 109
ankle 102
another 111
answer 111
ant 29
any 115
applaud 111
apple 102
area 109
arm 88
armor 108

army 98
around 115
as 115
ash 54
ask 29
at 54
athlete 61
attempt 29
away 115
awhile 94
baby 98
back 54
bake 63
bald 28
ball 108
balloon 109
balm 33
bank 38
barber 106
bask 54
bat 20
beach 41
beam 72
bear 91
beautiful 105
because 115
become 108
been 115
beg 20
bell 46
belt 28
bend 55
benign 33
berth 88
best 55
better 115
big 56
bill 20
billion 99
bind 67
bird 90
birth 89

biscuit 73
bitter 47
black 24
blanket 111
blast 54
blend 24
bless 46
blew 95
blimp 24
blind 67
blizzard 45
block 24
bloom 108
blotter 47
blouse 81
blow 82
bluff 46
blunt 24
boat 69
bob 57
boil 80
bold 68
boll 68
bolt 28
bond 29
bone 64
book 84
boot 74
booth 43
born 89
both 115
bow 81, 82
box 20
boy 78
bran 54
branch 37
brand 24
bread 72
break 73
breath 43
brick 24
brief 73
brig 24
bright 67
brim 24
bring 115
broad 72

broil 80
brook 84
broom 74
broth 43
brother 44
brown 81
brunt 24
brush 42
bubble 102
bud 20
buff 46
bug 58
build 73
bulk 28
bull 84
bump 29
bumper 106
burn 90
burr 46
burro 45
burst 90
bush 84
busy 47
butter 47
buy 115
buzz 46
by 97
cab 20
cactus 105
cafe 109
calf 111
call 115
calm 33
can 54
candle 102
captain 73
care 91
carpenter 106
carry 115
cash 42
cashier 109
cat 51
catch 38
cattle 47
caught 111
cave 63
cell 20

128

129

130

131

133

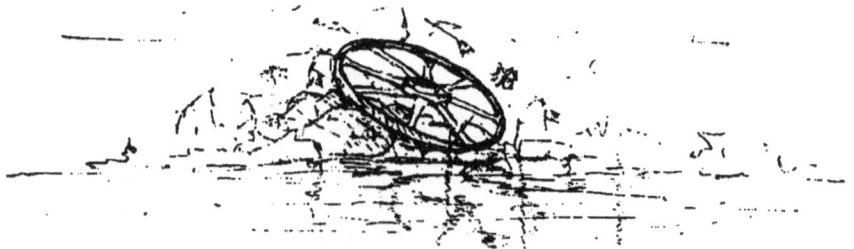